Steven Kellogg

FROGS JUMP

A COUNTING BOOK

by Alan Brooks

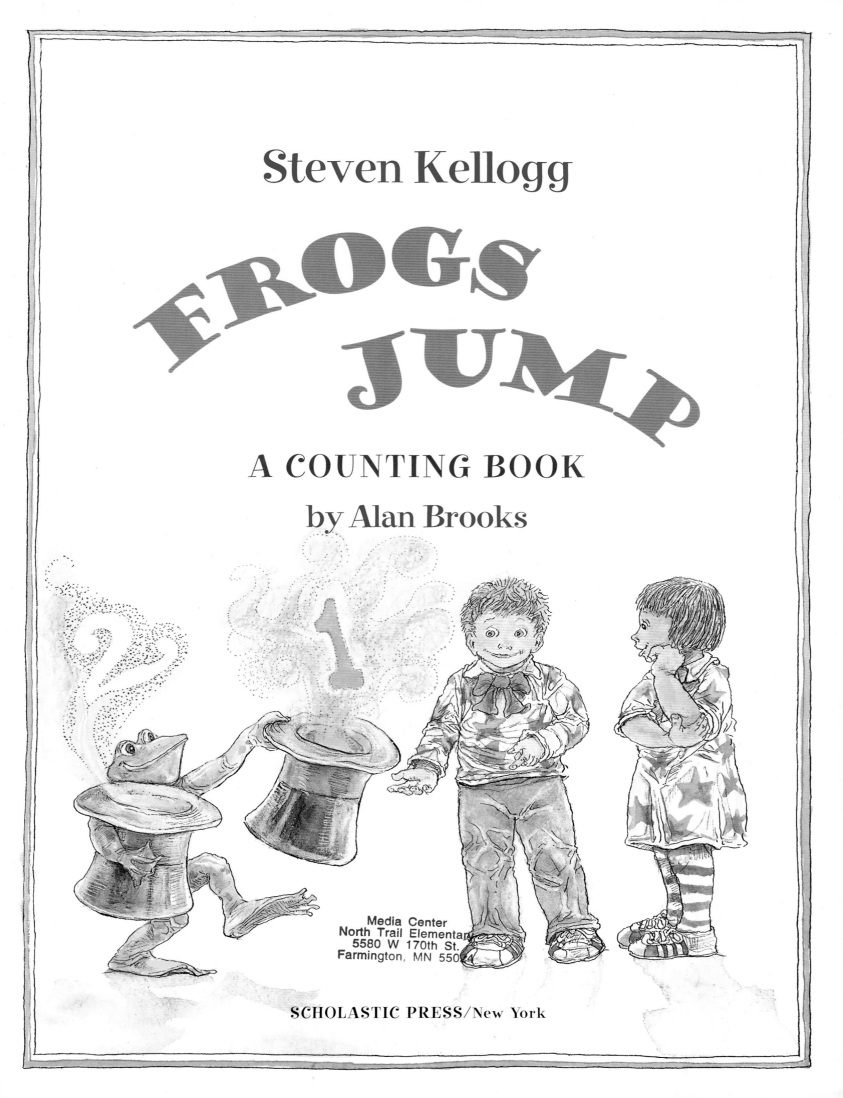

SCHOLASTIC PRESS/New York

Text copyright © 1996 by Alan Brooks   Illustrations copyright © 1996 by Steven Kellogg

All rights reserved. Published by Scholastic Press, a division of Scholastic Inc., *Publishers since 1920.*

No part of this publication may be reproduced or stored in a retrieval system or transmitted in any form or by any

means, electronic, mechanical, photocopying, recording, or otherwise, without written permission of the publisher.

For information regarding permission, please write to Scholastic Inc., 555 Broadway, New York, NY 10012.

Library of Congress Cataloging-in-Publication Data

Brooks, Alan, 1957-   Frogs jump / by Alan Brooks ; illustrated by Steven Kellogg.   p.   cm.

Summary: Illustrations provide humorous interpretations of the actions of animals from one frog to twelve whales.

ISBN 0-590-45528-1

[1. Animals—Fiction 2. Counting.]   I. Kellogg, Steven, ill.   II. Title.   PZ7.B78995Fr   1996   [E]—dc20   95-35917   CIP   AC

12 11 10 9 8 7 6 5 4 3 2 1   6 7 8 9/9 0 1/0   37

Printed in the U.S.A.   First printing, October 1996

The paintings in this book were executed in watercolor, colored inks, and acrylic on handmade watercolor paper.

The display type was set in Goudy Stout.   The text type was set in Elroy.

To CMT, for listening to all the frog jokes.
—A.B.

To super Sam Porter, with love.
—S.K.

One frog jumps.

One frog jumps, and two ducks dive.

One frog jumps, two ducks dive,

and **three** elephants trumpet.

One frog jumps, two ducks dive,
three elephants trumpet,
and four rabbits run.

One frog jumps, two ducks dive,
three elephants trumpet, four rabbits run,
and five bats bat.

One frog jumps, two ducks dive,
three elephants trumpet,
four rabbits run, five bats bat,
and six pelicans fish.

One frog jumps, two ducks dive,
three elephants trumpet, four rabbits run,
five bats bat, six pelicans fish,
and seven geese honk.

One frog jumps, two ducks dive,
three elephants trumpet, four rabbits run,
five bats bat,

six pelicans fish,
seven geese honk,
and **eight** monkeys swing.

One frog jumps, two ducks dive,
three elephants trumpet, four rabbits run,
five bats bat,

six pelicans fish,
seven geese honk, eight monkeys swing,
and nine spiders spin.

One frog jumps, two ducks dive,
three elephants trumpet, four rabbits run,
five bats bat, six pelicans fish,

seven geese honk,
eight monkeys swing, nine spiders spin,
and ten snakes slide.

One frog jumps, **two** ducks dive,
three elephants trumpet, **four** rabbits run,
five bats bat, **six** pelicans fish,

seven geese honk, **eight** monkeys swing,
nine spiders spin, **ten** snakes slide,
and **eleven** pigs squeal.

HONK
HONK
HONK
HONK
HONK
HONK
HONK
HONK
HONK

HONK
MOBILE

One frog jumps, two ducks dive,
three elephants trumpet, four rabbits run,
five bats bat, six pelicans fish, seven geese honk,

eight monkeys swing, nine spiders spin,
ten snakes slide, eleven pigs squeal,
and twelve whales blow soap bubbles.

What? Whales
don't blow
soap bubbles!

Whales
don't
blow
soap
bubbles?

Whales don't blow soap bubbles.

Pigs don't squeal on motorcycles.

Snakes don't slide on waterslides.

Spiders don't spin on the merry-go-round.

Monkeys don't swing golf clubs.

Geese don't honk car horns.

Pelicans don't fish with poles.

Bats don't bat birdies.

Rabbits don't run in sneakers.

Elephants don't play trumpets.

Ducks don't dive off diving boards.

But frogs. . .

ANY WAY
THEY WANT!